# David Del Tredici
# Mandango

Five Gay-Themed Pieces
for Piano

BOOSEY & HAWKES

AN IMAGEM COMPANY

DISTRIBUTED BY

HAL•LEONARD®
CORPORATION
7777 W. BLUEMOUND RD. P.O. BOX 13819 MILWAUKEE, WI 53213

www.boosey.com
www.halleonard.com

Published by Boosey & Hawkes, Inc.
229 West 28<sup>th</sup> Street, 11<sup>th</sup> Floor
New York NY 10001

www.boosey.com

 AN IMAGEM COMPANY

Computer music setting by Steven Burke and David Nadal

ISMN: 979-0-051-24662-5

First performed on September 2, 2009 at Bargemusic, New York City
David Del Tredici, piano


CONTENTS

SAME–SEX MARRIAGE ........................1

LGBT........................................13

IN MEMORIAM, A. C. ...........................20

MUMMIFICATION.................................27

MANDANGO. ...........................................30

1. Same–Sex Marriage – 4' 30"
2. LGBT – 4'
3. In Memoriam, A.C. – 4'
4. Mummification – 3'
5. Mandango – 11'


Total duration: ca. 26' 30" – played without pause

# COMPOSER'S NOTES

**MANDANGO**—5 pieces played without pause—is the latest in my series of works celebrating the gay experience in all its diversity.

**"Same-sex Marriage"** begins with fast, canonically-chasing lines, moves to a more lyrical middle section, there returns to the bustle of the opening when there suddenly appears, chorale prelude-like, a quotation from a famous wedding march. This grows to a climax, then retreats. In the ensuing quiet, another familiar wedding march begins tentatively, then grows to an even grander climax. All the while the breathless music from the beginning swirls in joyous counterpoint.

**"LGBT"** (Lesbian, Gay, Bisexual, Transgender) is based on notes derived from this acronym. L is *la,* T is *ti* or B. The notes A, G, B, B then are the theme in the gentle opening section. The music wanders quickly through many keys—perhaps a musical equivalent of diversity. A more passionate middle section follows and leads to a recapitulation, then a tiny coda.

**"In Memoriam, A. C."** The A. C. initialized here is, of course, Aaron Copland—a dear friend and mentor. The notes and even the rhythm are derived from his name: A, A, C, A, D are the musical letters found there. The rhythm is dictated by the varying and precise distances between each of these musical letters and the non-musical letters: AAron CoplAnD.

Static and quietly atonal, this music moves in 16 measure units that go from slow to fast. These units are punctuated by seemingly random *forte* chords. Only at the end, when, in tribute, Copland's famous Shaker melody is added, are these chords revealed as the tune's accompaniment. At the same time, in counterpoint, is heard the Copland motto AACAD.

**"Mummification"** In the world of S/M, (Sado Masochism) mummification means to mummify. That is, to completely wrap a person in some kind of tape (Saran Wrap will do!), place him in a quiet place, and allow him to have whatever experience he will. This short piece is a succession of slowly moving quarter-note chords. The dynamic level is always *pianissimo.* The mood is one of hushed tenderness. Only at the end, does the rhythm change—but gently.

**"Mandango"** At 11 minutes, this is the big piece of the set. *Mandango* is a gayish corruption of the word fandango—a tango-like dance of sensuality and sexiness. Along the way, there are points of musical interest. Each time the main theme reappears, the musical pulse quickens. At the start the music moves in quarter-notes—then in dotted eighths—then eighths—then sixteenths. Finally, it reaches a frenzy of still faster triplet sixteenth notes. Separating these gradually accelerating recapitulations are various contrasting sections, the most developed of these is a fugue.

But this is only half of the piece; once the opening music has reached this frenzied, fastest tempo, it dissipates, and becomes background for an entirely new and contrasting theme—one more graceful and innocent. The development of this new theme, however, is interrupted by bursts from the previously heard, frenzy–music.

Finally – as if to nail it down once and for all – a slower, *molto cantabile* statement of the new theme appears. But, once again, uncontrollably, the music begins to speed up, sweeping all before it into a coda full of pianistic glory and *martellato* octaves.

Each piece, except for *In Memoriam A. C.,* is dedicated to gay couple friends (and a nephew) of mine: I. John Corigliano & Marc Adamo, II. Bill Christ & Gary DiPasquale, IV. Aaron Del Tredici & John Van, and V. Marc Peloquin & Seth Slade.

—David Del Tredici

# MANDANGO

## I. SAME-SEX MARRIAGE

*for John Corigliano and Mark Adamo*

DAVID DEL TREDICI

Allegro (♩. = 112)

979-0-051-24662-5

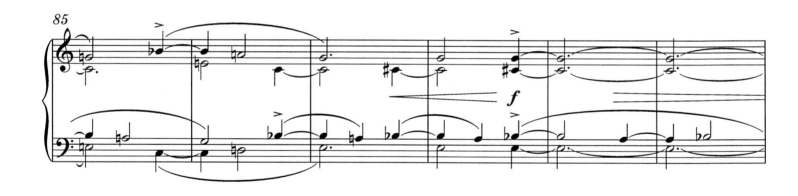

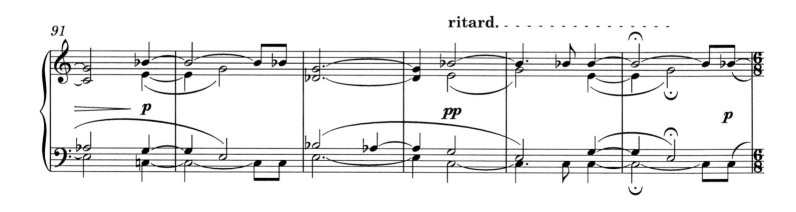

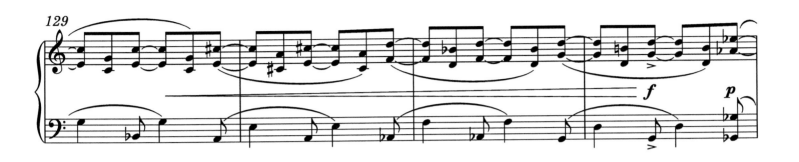

I. Same-Sex Marriage

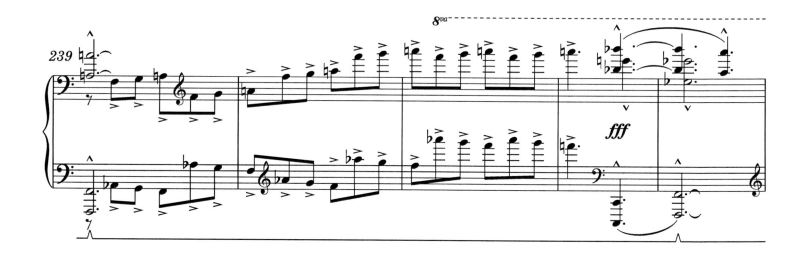

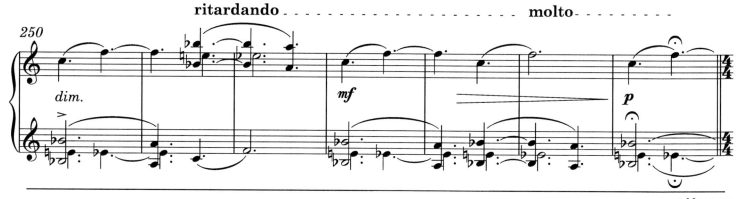

**attacca**

July 13–15, 2008
Seattle, Washington / New York City

# II. LGBT

*for Bill Crist and Gary DiPasquale*

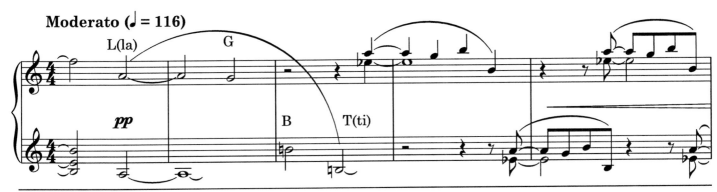

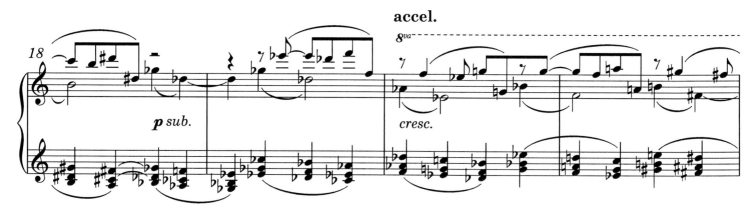

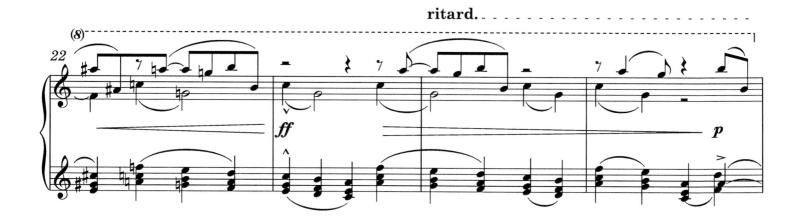

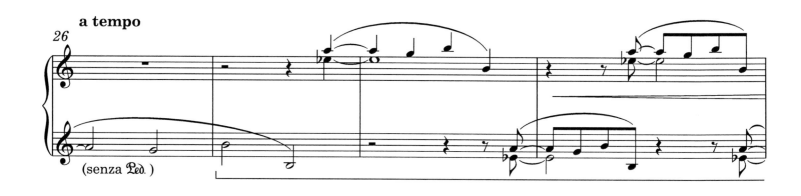

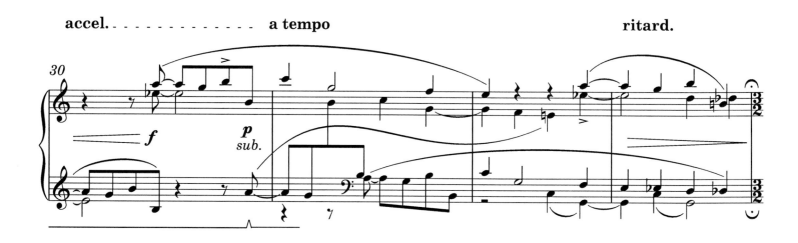

**Più mosso** (♩ = 92)

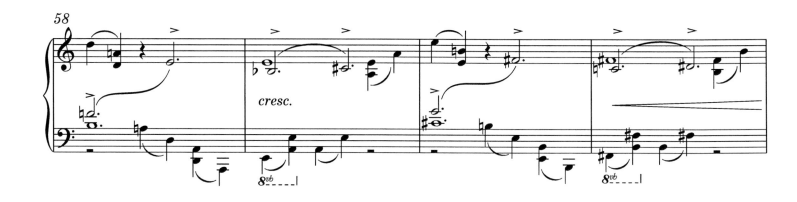

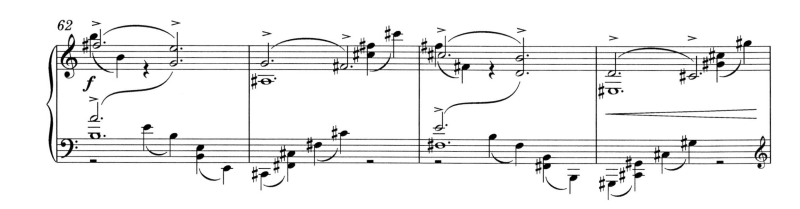

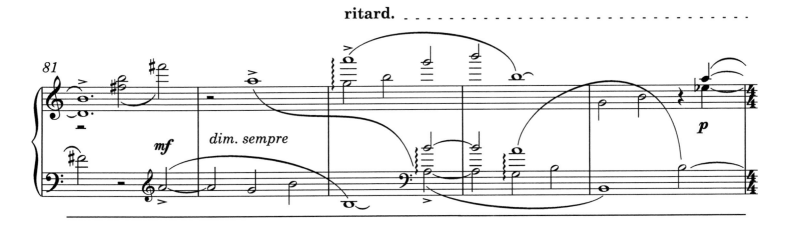

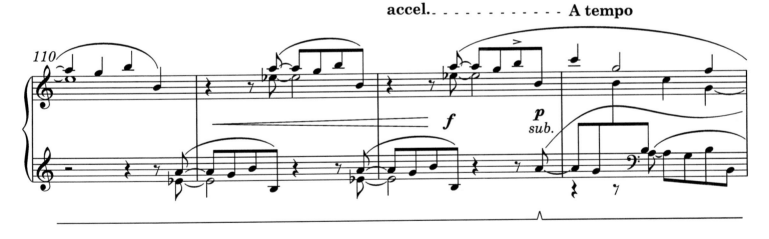

July 19–24, 2008
Eugene, Oregon / New York City

# III. IN MEMORIAM, A.C.

**Andante (♩. = 100)**

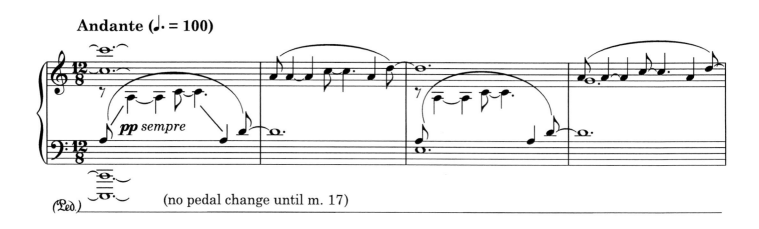

*pp sempre*

(Ped.)  (no pedal change until m. 17)

*cresc.*

III. In Memoriam, A.C.

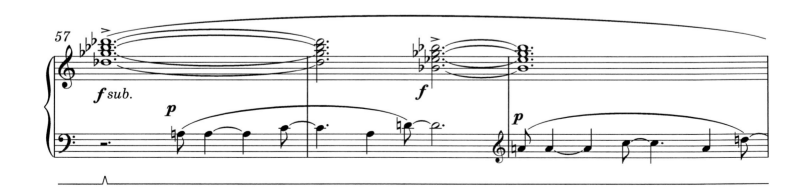

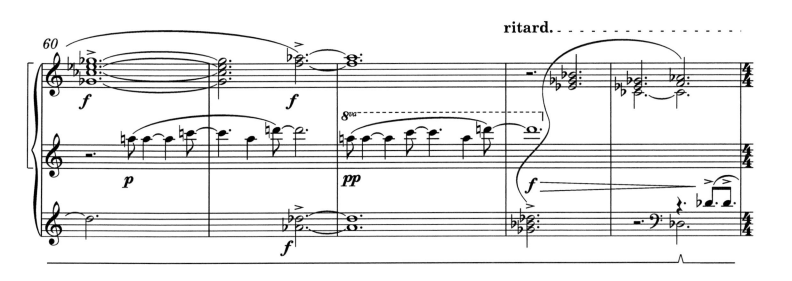

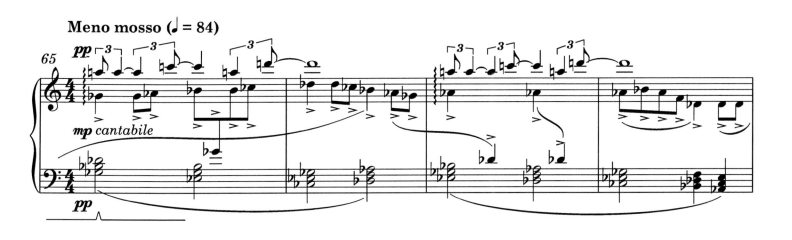

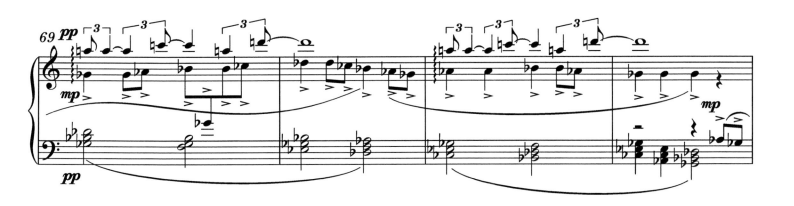

III. In Memoriam, A.C.

attacca

August 3–6, 2008
New York City

# IV. MUMMIFICATION

*for Aaron Del Tredici and John Van*

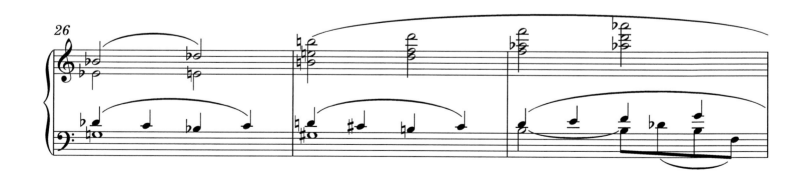

August 8–9, 2008
New York City

# V. MANDANGO

*for Marc Peloquin and Seth Slade*

V. Mandango

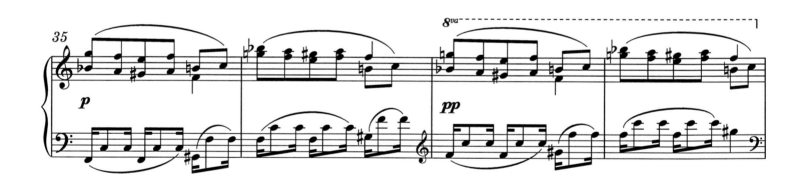

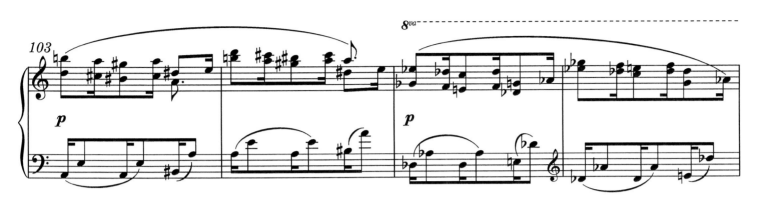

V. Mandango

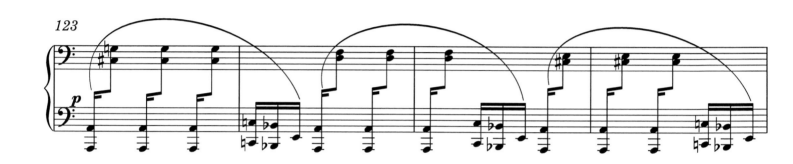

**133 FUGA:**

V. Mandango

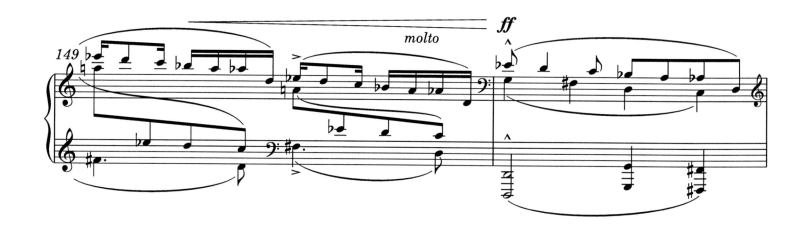

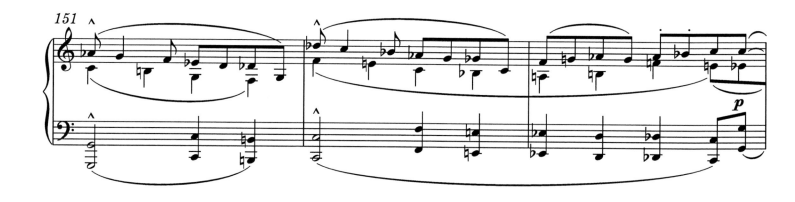

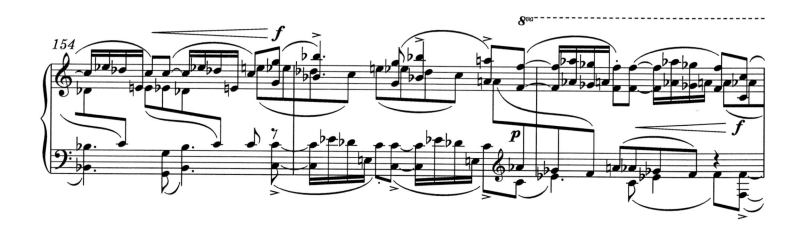

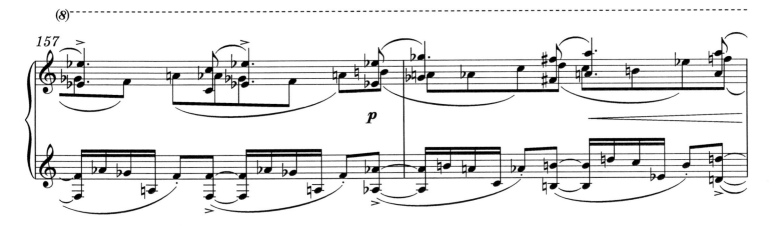

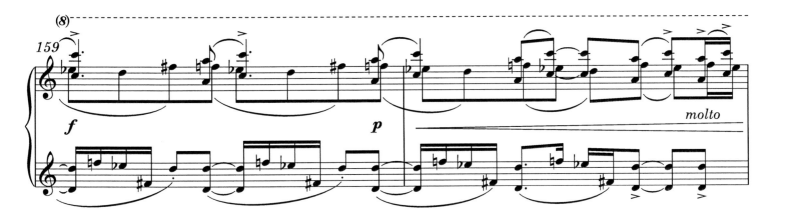

V. Mandango

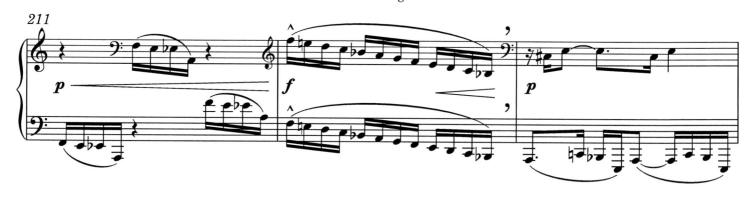

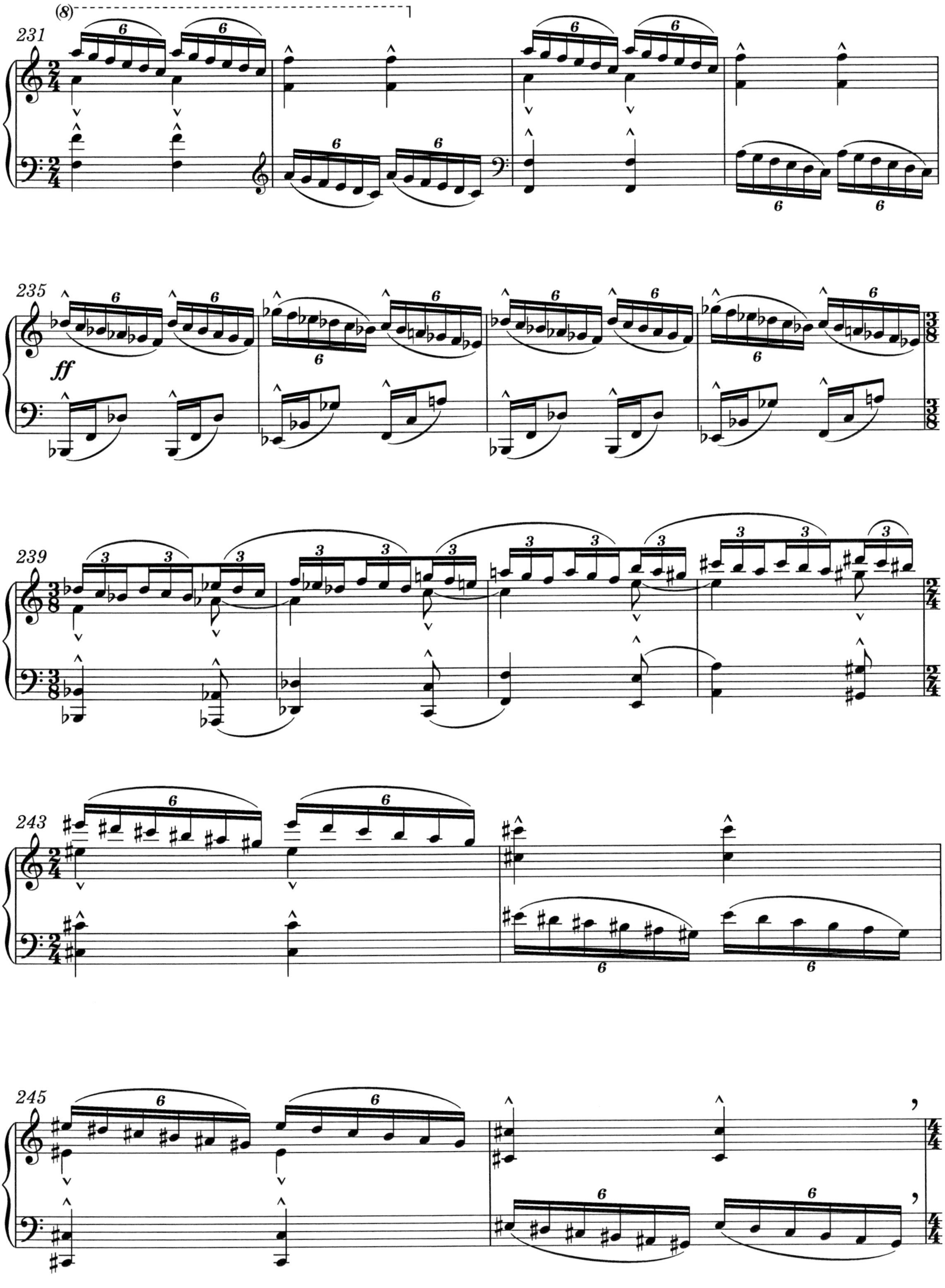
(8)
231
235
ff
239
243
245

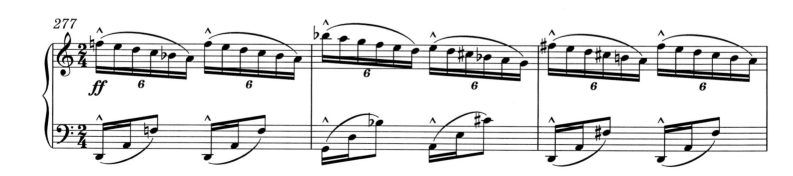

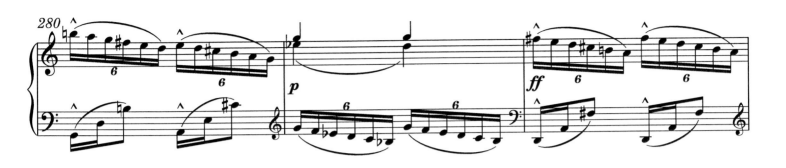

V. Mandango

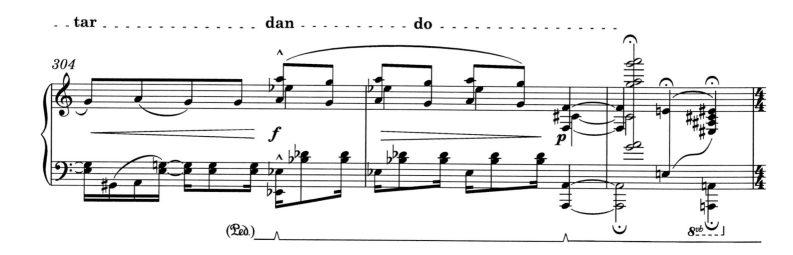

**Meno mosso, amoroso**

V. Mandango

V. Mandango

V. Mandango

ritard. - - - - - - - - - - - - - poco - - - - - - - - - - - - - a - - - - - - - - poco - - - - -

- - - - - - - - - - - - - - - - - - - - - molto ritard. - - - - - - - - - - - - - - - - - - - -